THE L
SPIDER

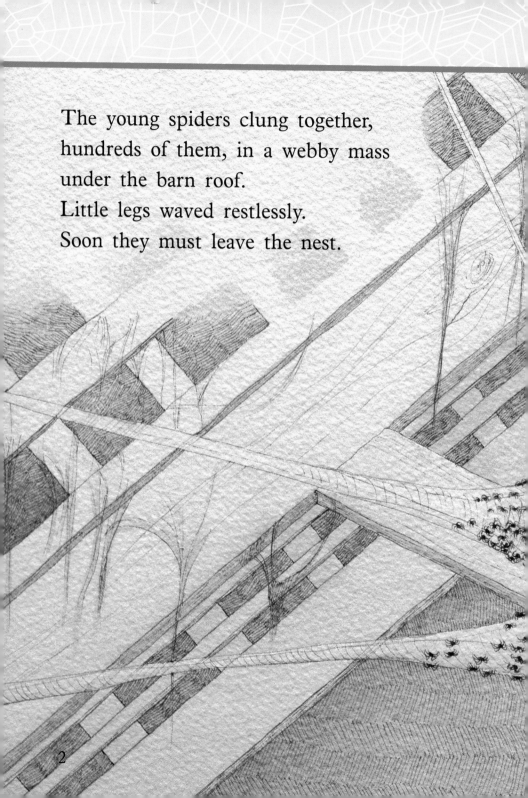

The young spiders clung together,
hundreds of them, in a webby mass
under the barn roof.
Little legs waved restlessly.
Soon they must leave the nest.

3

At last, one little spider began to climb.
Up the roof she climbed,
on her eight tiny legs,
until she could get no higher.
Then she stopped.
She waited.
The air was just right,
not too still, not too windy.
It was time to go.

The little spider began to spin a fine thread.
One, two, three silky lines
floated out behind her.
Then she let go of the roof
and they lifted her high into the air.

The little spider flew a long way
in her search for a new home.
First she came to a tall tree.
She drew in her lines
and landed on the top branch.
This would be a good place to live.

Thump! A big blackbird landed on the branch,
and she nearly fell off.
The bird's bright eyes spotted the tiny spider,
but before it could eat her,
she scuttled under a leaf.
She hid under a tiny crack
until the bird flew away.
The tree was not a good place to live.

The little spider let out her silky lines
and floated away on the wind,
until down below, she saw a house.
She pulled in the lines,
drifted down,
and floated in through an open window.
She hid behind the curtain.
This was a good place to live.

Swish! A big feather duster whisked her away.
In another moment,
she was being shaken out of the window
on the end of the duster.
Quickly, she swung on her lines,
landed on the drainpipe, and hung on.
The window was not a good place to live.
She climbed down the drainpipe
and hid inside it, at the bottom.
It was cool and dark in the pipe.
It might be a good place to live.

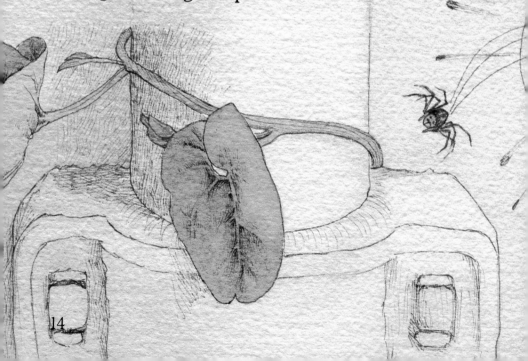

Woosh! A sudden rush of water
came down the pipe.
It swept the little spider out of the pipe,
into the drain.
She held on tightly with all eight legs.
When at last the water stopped,
she was very wet.
The pipe was not a good place to live.

The little spider crawled out of the drain
and dragged herself across the yard.
She was very tired.
She climbed up a big tractor wheel
and hid in the dark at the top.
This could be a good place to live.

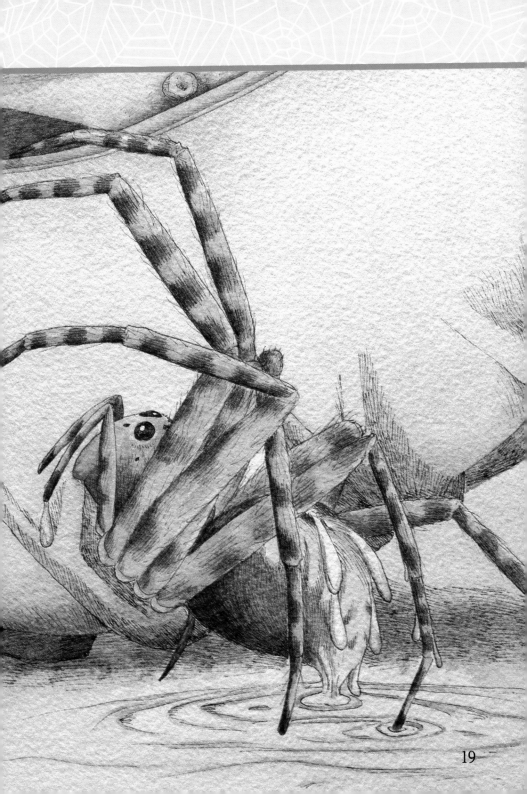

Then such a noise began—
such a rumbling and shaking!
The wheels began to turn.
The tractor was moving.
The little spider hung on
and hoped it would stop before she fell off.
It was not a good place to live.

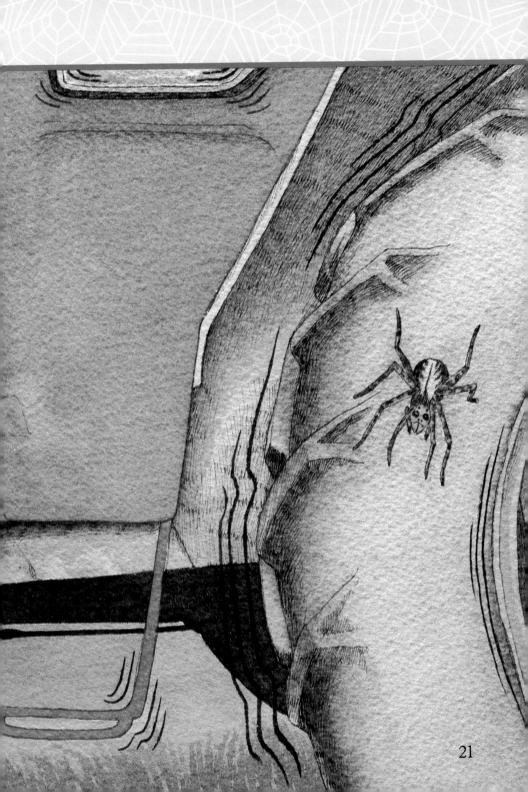

At last, the tractor stopped.
It was in a barn.
The farmer jumped down,
shut the barn doors,
and went away.
The little spider crawled out.

The barn was dark and dusty.
It looked like home.
It smelled like home.
She began to climb.
Up she went, until she was high up
in the roof of the barn –
safe from birds,
and dusters,
and water,
and noisy machines.
This was a good home.